Spaces for Growth: learning our way out of a crisis

Graham Leicester
and Maureen O'Hara

This project is the result of a collaboration between Koreo and International Futures Forum, and was funded by Koreo as part of their ongoing inquiry into how to create and hold the most powerful learning spaces for social change. It is also published as a series on the Koreo medium.

"A person lives not only their personal life, as an individual, but also, consciously or unconsciously, the life of their epoch and their contemporaries."
Thomas Mann, *The Magic Mountain*, 1924

"We do not solve our problems, we outgrow them."
Carl Jung, *Collected Works*, 1938

Published by Triarchy Press, Axminster, UK
www.triarchypress.net
admin@triarchypress.net

A catalogue record for this book is available from the British Library.

ISBNs
Print: 978-1-913743-46-8
eBook: 978-1-913743-47-5

Design and illustration by Phil Arthur
philarthur.co.uk

Contents

Introduction

Nobody picking up this booklet in the shadow of a violent geopolitical crisis, an ongoing global pandemic, dangerous climate change and numerous other worrying trends needs any reminding that we live in powerful times.

They are both challenging and revealing. Arundhati Roy captured the imagination in early April 2020 when she wrote about "the pandemic as portal" to a better world. But she also described it as a rupture, "an opportunity to rethink the doomsday machine".

In normal times we tend to go about our lives largely oblivious to the structures, institutions, processes and shared values that shape our behaviours. Like the iceberg, most of this lies invisible below the surface. We can see more clearly now. Deep structures of love, power and justice have been brought to light and social/political patterns of great strain are on display for all to see.

There are more proximate challenges too. The global public health crisis is far from over. The economic consequences will play out over at least a decade, to say nothing of other pressing issues starved of attention, locally and globally, while we have concentrated our efforts on responding to Coronavirus. This is the landscape of recovery and renewal.

My organisation, International Futures Forum (IFF), has for some time been tracking three emergencies: a real emergency (the challenges we face in the world), a conceptual emergency (making sense of the world to take on those challenges) and an existential emergency (how all of this leaves us feeling at a human level).

These are not distinct: they are all connected. Yet as the pandemic has unfolded and our capacity to thrive in a landscape of deep uncertainty and profound loss has been tested, it is the existential emergency, the human consequences of living in powerful times, that has dominated the scene.

That is the subject of this booklet. For it is in the boundless potential of the human system, the ways in which we choose to live our lives in patterns of relationship with other lives, that our hopes for a better future ultimately lie. Learning how to draw that potential from us, individually and collectively, is an urgent task – one that IFF, Koreo and we hope many others are ready to take on.

Together we need to support individuals, groups, organisations, communities, institutions, human beings in all formations to expand, to develop and to grow, to rise to the occasion.

At heart this is a learning journey in three steps

The first step is awareness. We can expand our natural capacities to appreciate more of what is going on around us. We can learn to feel at home in a confusing and uncertain landscape rather than constantly buffeted and overwhelmed. We are born to live in this environment. We are a part of it. We – as individuals, and certainly collectively – are at least as complex as the circumstances whirling around us. We have been disrupted, knocked off balance, pitched into an unfamiliar, uncertain, fast-changing and contested landscape. We need to pause, reflect, look around, come to our senses, find our feet.

The second step is transformative growth. Just because we can read the landscape does not mean we necessarily know how to inhabit it, still less how to influence it. We know that as human beings we have tremendous potential and often surprise ourselves with our competence and capacity when pushed to the edge in times of crisis. What are the ways of knowing, being and being together that we need to develop to flourish and act effectively in these times?

The third step is action. Once we have it all together, we feel like confident participants rather than helpless victims in a turbulent world, and we have allowed the circumstances to bring forth and develop our innate 21st-century competencies to live well in this moment – how then should we act to address the crisis, respond to the emergencies, tackle the challenges and shift our systems to a better place? We need to act wisely and to act well.

The 21st century is a new culture, a world that has never existed before – we are all immigrants, many feel like refugees needing to adapt to a new world. For years IFF has been focused on understanding the deeper story of this new century and how we can create the enabling spaces where inherent human creative competencies can be set free to explore and build the emerging culture – where new 21st-century ways of being, knowing, doing and being together can be realised.[1]

---

[1] See the brief appendix on page 56 for further details of this work and other useful references.

This booklet is another contribution to that work. It is written with and for Koreo and its partners. We have high hopes that through our joint efforts, and the work of other like-minded organisations, we will see much greater ease of access to the kinds of spaces for human growth and development discussed here: conversational spaces, civic spaces, virtual spaces, work spaces, learning spaces. Who knows, perhaps in time these principles will start to infiltrate our formal structures of education, and even our politics.

Our goal is to enable 21st-century people to become artists of their own lives, in supportive patterns of relationship with others, doing meaningful work, offering practical hope.

If we are to rise to the challenge of this century we will need all of this and all of us: revealing the abundance that lies in our humanity and the full magnificence of the human being.

Outline

The structure of the booklet broadly follows the three steps already described: awareness, transformative growth and action.

The first section explores the context of our times and how we can learn to read the landscape more effectively, coming to feel more at home in it.

The second section focuses on transformative growth, both what we need to develop in ourselves – the 21st-century competencies – and how we can do so. This includes a detailed discussion of the kinds of 'spaces' (literal and metaphorical, physical and virtual) we need to create and maintain to encourage such growth and the hosts and guides required to 'hold' them.

The third section moves to action, in particular transformative action that will shift our systems and patterns of activity towards our aspirations for the future. It focuses on the skills of the producer, working effectively in the midst of turmoil and uncertainty to realise ambitious, culture-shifting intentions. Practical hope.

The message of the booklet is that we already have all we need. That is the wonder of the human system. A brief final section encourages readers to get into action (including by drawing on some simple first moves and sources of support listed in the appendix). Its message is: start where you are.

Book Structure

STEP 1
Awareness

3 EMERGENCIES

Real   Conceptual   Existential

3 RESPONSES

Defensive Denial   Collapse   Growth

3 LITERACIES

Psychological   Cultural   Knowledge

Transformative Growth

4 ARENAS

Expansion, Development and Growth
We Are Already Competent
The Core Stance
The Facilitating Environment

6 SPACES

Safe (Enough)
Empty
Reflective
Expansive
Liminal
Prophetic

STEP 3

Transformative Action

7 PRACTICES

Don't start from "this is impossible"
There are no rules
Get the fears articulated
Make friends
Take responsibility and seek contribution
Don't ask for permission – it cannot be given
Push the ambition

Section One:

The First Step Is Awareness

Powerful Times

"We are always here"

In 2005 our friend Eamonn Kelly wrote a book called *Powerful Times*. It was about the future, which we have always seen 'through a glass, darkly'. With our eyes accustomed to the gloom, might it be possible, he asked, to see the way ahead just a little more clearly?

The short answer was no. Every plausible, evidence-rich, internally consistent and compelling version of the emerging future Kelly found could be matched with an equally plausible, evidence-rich, internally consistent and compelling story of a pathway leading in precisely the opposite direction.

It is a glorious condition of life itself. Contingency and indeterminacy is of the essence. As Iona Heath, a remarkable doctor who thinks deeply not just about quantity but also about quality of life, says, "Only because we do not understand everything and because we cannot control the future is it possible to live and to be human."

At the same time, too much uncertainty can be disconcerting, even overwhelming. Kelly's book takes its title from an episode in the turbulent times of the Renaissance. Pandolfo Petrucci, Lord of Siena, was challenged by Machiavelli on his inconstant, confusing and frankly suspicious behaviour. His response was simple and disarming: "Wishing to make as few mistakes as possible, I arrange my affairs hour by hour, because the times are more powerful than our brains."

That description surely resonates for many of us today. We live in a 'VUCA world', an ugly but now pervasive shorthand – volatile, uncertain, complex, ambiguous. A tangle of interconnected challenges, horsemen of the apocalypse, black swans, synchronous failures, cascading collapses and much more.

We have been living with these threats for some time. A global pandemic, for example, has been sitting at or close to the top of the global 'risk register' for at least a decade – alongside many other equally worrying and ultimately connected challenges.

We can do better than Petrucci. We know more. We have learned more about human capacity and ingenuity, especially in crisis. We can manage our confusion without tuning out the creative, life-giving energy of contingency, imagination and the unknown. We can learn to 'keep calm' – as all those wartime posters and their parodies tell us – not just to carry on, but to grow and adapt and expand into the challenges we face.

It was heartening then, in a call with three senior Scottish Government officials soon after the Coronavirus pandemic broke and the UK went into lockdown, to find a calm acceptance, even recognition.

Unlike the Lord of Siena, these people had their wits about them. They were not going to let themselves be overwhelmed, nor did they mistake this crisis for the last one.

They knew they were being drawn deeper into the tangle, but they were ready, not spooked. As one of them said early in the conversation: "We are always here. And we have been here before."

Three Emergencies

An emergency arises out of emergence – trends gather pace, reach a tipping point, trigger disruption, interruption or worse, and feed off each other in unexpected ways that threaten to overwhelm us.

It is helpful to discern three distinct modes, interlinked and mutually reinforcing. The global pandemic has made each one of these modes more obvious, more visible and more intense.

There is clearly a real emergency (or a 'visible' or 'manifest' emergency – they are all real): the incipient breakdown of systems we used to take for granted, from democratic governance and decision-making to ecological balance, the persistence of poverty, inequality and injustice which threaten social cohesion, the challenge of maintaining basic universal services like health care or clean water, cumulative carbon emissions triggering a 'climate emergency'. And so on. The list is familiar and daunting.

At the same time there is a conceptual emergency: the pervading sense of cognitive dissonance experienced when the core concepts we have relied on to make sense of our world are no longer up to the task. We are confused. We don't know what to believe any more. The ways of thinking and acting we have relied on in the past are no longer effective, or are even counter-productive. Our problems are showing up as paradoxes or intractable conundrums. We don't know what to do, we have no faith in any of the 'solutions' on offer, but we must do something. This is a conceptual emergency.

The real and the conceptual emergencies are also felt in an existential emergency, in which their effects show up at the level of the human being, individually and collectively. Going deeper than cognitive frames and schemas, identity itself is threatened. The shared narratives and patterns of life which provide the 'glue' that hold individuals, communities and societies together start coming apart. Societies become incoherent and fragmented, experiencing 'culture wars', a loosening of cultural solidarity and a loss of faith in shared institutions. Individuals can no longer make constructive, coherent sense of the lives they are living – where to settle, what to do next, how to live. Our collective sanity and sense of continuing existence as a species on a liveable planet is cast in doubt.

These emergencies have been with us for a while. What has changed over time, and which the seismic disruption of the pandemic has highlighted, is the intensity – and indeed the extensity – of these three emergencies.

They now hunt in packs.

The annual *World Economic Forum Global Risks Report* for 2020, for example, registers only real emergencies: climate action failure, weapons of mass destruction, extreme weather, water crises, cyber-attacks, infectious diseases and so on.

Dig a little deeper, however, and each one reveals its roots in conceptual confusion and complexity; each one relates to, and impacts on, all the others; each one reflects recent trends in big data, fake news and an erosion of trust in the agencies responsible for providing reliable information and keeping us safe.

Each is also starting to show existential impact, contributing to rising levels of mental distress in most countries and cultures across the world – showing up in sleep problems, anxiety and depression, suicidal thoughts and behaviours, addictions, violence, relationship and family breakdown, the 'diseases of despair'.

No wonder we go to such elaborate, often unconscious, lengths to keep acknowledgement of the real emergencies at bay.

But now the defensive bubble is burst. It is impossible to ignore the ravages of the Coronavirus pandemic across the planet, the harsh spotlight it has cast on structural poverty, inequality and racism, the prospect of economic disruption for years to come, the unravelling of consensual reasoning and even collective sanity.

Here we are. We are always here. And we have been here before.

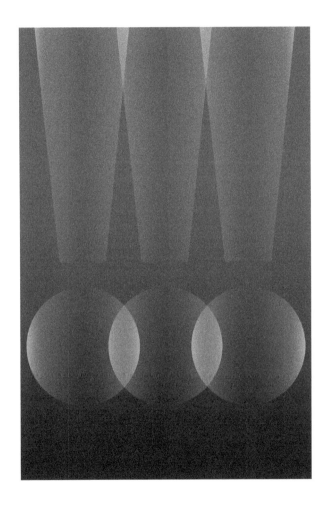

Coming to our Senses

Three Responses

Just as there are three emergencies, so we also see – at a human level – three typical responses.

One is defensive denial. This is the most common. We refuse to acknowledge that things have changed and strive to maintain the comfort of control and coherence by reasserting old truths with more conviction and urgency. We stress fundamentals, ignore inconvenient information, rationalise, blame others, deflect, interpret complexity in simple terms.

These strategies are mostly unconscious and are a default defence against too much unsettling information and rising psychological uncertainty. Because they are unconscious, we usually believe the distorted view of reality they present and are hard to persuade to any other point of view.

Denial can offer temporary comfort in new circumstances and will quell anxiety for a while until stability returns. But if it needs to be maintained over a prolonged period, the costs in psychological effort and energy mount. We become easy prey for despotic leaders, vulnerable to anyone or anything promising the restoration of certainty, simplicity and recovery of the familiar.

A second response is collapse. It usually follows the first, as the effort involved in tuning out reality eventually becomes too much and gives way. The result is not a return to good sense, but rather the opposite. Again largely unconsciously, people fall into a delusional or fantasy world where they make up a reality that is tolerable for them, however distorted it might be.

In that unreal world they can give up the struggle to make sense of the complexities around them, lose themselves in their fear and rage, grasp whatever conspiracy theory allows them to hang on, secure in their delusional belief that they will be fine even in a world they see as full of threats and hidden dangers. The collapse can come suddenly, like an avalanche, or as a slow slide into decay. This is a dangerous, psychotic level of defence against unbearable levels of anxiety.

If these responses were all that is available to cope with powerful times, the human species would have perished long before now. Fortunately, beyond denial and collapse, there is another response possible.

We can as individual persons[2] or in groups adopt a more growth-oriented stance, neither denying nor tuning out the confusing and overwhelming complexity we experience. We can sit with the messiness, engage with it, develop and grow through it.

---

[2] We use the word 'persons' in the technical sense that the psychologist Carl Rogers used it, to represent an individual in relationship with others rather than an atomised individual. There will be more on this important distinction in chapter 4.

In some situations, when conditions are right, we can transcend the apparent chaos and expand into something genuinely new. We adapt to the times not as they are but as they are becoming, allowing the new circumstances to call forth capacities, individually and collectively, that we did not know we possessed. This is the growth response and it is transformative.

We are human beings. We can grow. Given the right conditions and support, we rise to the occasion.

The first step is awareness.

Three Literacies

If we are to move beyond denial or confusion, restore ourselves as agents rather than passive victims of circumstance, we must first become more conscious and skilful in reading and sensing the landscape we inhabit.

Roger Federer is a remarkably graceful tennis player. Like many great sportspeople he has learned through experience to read the game in all its complexity so that, even when playing at speed, he seems to have more time on the ball. His experience allows him to sense where the ball is going next and how it might arrive. At his best he was always in position ahead of time, ready to respond, seemingly unhurried even in such a fast-paced game.

We need to learn to do the same in our own fast-changing environment. 'Time on the ball' in our context, getting a sense of the landscape, how it is unfolding and what might be coming next, gives us the opportunity for conscious reflection on what we are doing, how we are being. It prevents overwhelm and enables us skilfully to respond to events – even getting a few moves ahead of them – rather than just reacting to them.

We can start by improving our natural capacity to read our environment using three literacies: psychology, culture and knowledge.

Psychological Literacy

We all have inner lives, an unconscious or at least a sub-conscious dimension to our behaviours of which we are usually unaware. We can choose, consciously, to pay attention.

Noticing, reading and interpreting the psychological dimension of the landscape is a capacity we call 'psychological literacy'. It allows us to perceive, recognise, feel and interpret our own and others' psychological experiences as they occur, moment by moment, and spontaneously adjust our behaviour in response to that perception.

This gives us the option of moving beyond the default defence of denial and withdrawal as psychological protection against anxiety. We can engage with reality rather than deny it, drawing on other psychological resources and invoking a transformative growth response.

We can summon a spirit of hope, courage, invention and play and bring them consciously into the mix, in the moment, not in a rehearsed or rule-based way. We can become actively reflective, conscious of the impact of actions and inactions even as we are performing them. That capacity too can be calibrated – so that we don't become paralysed by too much reflection, like the athlete who 'chokes' through thinking too much.

This capacity for self-awareness, for poise and grace in action, is widely regarded as the beginning of wisdom and of mastery. This is the first protection against denial as a default response to overwhelm – and thus the pathway to learning and growth.

Cultural Literacy

We can also read our environment through a cultural lens. We are, and always have been, encultured beings.

Until the modern era in the West, and it is still the case in many of the world's cultures, individuals lived their entire lives within one cultural context. From cradle to grave they were immersed in, and shaped by, societies that were deeply coherent. The expectation was that children should be socialised to understand and conform to the givens of life in that society. Those givens covered all that was expected for a successful life.

Culture in that context became invisible, like the water we swim in. In powerful times we require a more conscious awareness of culture: an active acknowledgement that we are always operating inside a cultural context, usually today not in one but in many, and that most of those cultures are now shaken and in flux.

In the globally connected 21st century every act has cultural significance. Most of us are blind to all but the most obvious. But some people develop a subtle cultural awareness, which allows them to feel at home in a hybrid, shifting, multifarious culture that denies us more traditional sources of stability and identity.

'Cultural literacy' is the capacity to perceive, understand and participate fluently within a culture that shapes us while knowing there are also other cultures. It gives us the opportunity to be able to meet those other cultures gracefully and respectfully and to transgress cultural norms with conscious subtlety and respect when that is called for. It also helps us understand that every intervention within a human system is a cultural intervention, it inevitably carries a culture with it.

Knowledge Literacy

Events of recent years have forced the issue of epistemology and worldview – what counts as knowledge and how we know what we know – out of the rarefied world of philosophy into ordinary everyday life. What are we to make of disagreements over 'the science' in relation to our pandemic response, or the White House's famous insistence on 'alternative facts'? We all now need to develop our capacity to read the deeper frames underpinning what constitutes knowledge in any situation, recognising there are many perspectives on what counts as 'truth', some more reliable than others.

We need to be aware of how knowledge is created in diverse knowledge landscapes and disciplines – economics, botany, psychology, poetry, politics, gardening, dance – and how difficult it is to weigh any one against the measure of the others.

Many of us of a certain age when asked 'what is the meaning of life?' automatically answer '42'. Douglas Adams' famous joke has penetrated into popular culture. It turns precisely on our innate awareness of different ways of knowing which, while complete and reliable in themselves, are fundamentally incommensurable. Life is not an equation.

Knowledge literacy allows us to recognise these multiple systems of arriving at truth, to make the commitment to our own 'truths' more tentative and therefore open to new knowledge. It reminds us fundamentally that 'objective' knowledge derived from abstraction and reasoning is just one way of knowing and one kind of truth. Especially in the social sphere, objective truth claims are no more or less 'valid' than 'subjective' knowledge gained from our own unique lived experience or the 'felt' knowledge that lives in the body. All of these channels are ways of making sense of our world – we can open them all if we choose, and at least become more aware of our assumptions about 'validity' and trust.

Together, enhanced psychological, cultural and knowledge literacy give us an expanded capacity for reading the complex landscape of our lives. These literacies allow us to be in the messiness without being overwhelmed by it. They help us find our feet, come to our senses, and prepare for more effective action.

The arc of the moral universe may be long and bending towards justice (as Martin Luther King Jr put it) – but it helps if we can read the emerging landscape with sufficient clarity to know how and where and when to put our shoulder to the wheel.

Section Two:
Transformative Growth

21st-Century Competencies

Expansion, Development and Growth

Reading the landscape, continuously reflecting on it, we start to feel at home in it: comfortable in complexity. We are no longer flotsam and jetsam tossed on the tide of events. We feel like agents, active participants in the landscape.

If the first step is awareness, the second – given the right conditions and support – will be expansion, development and growth.

We will see that we are able to shape and influence the landscape through our own actions and should be able to move through it skilfully and with intention. So what skills, capacities, competencies might we now need to develop in order to act wisely and live well?

In 1993 UNESCO established an international Commission, chaired by Jacques Delors, to investigate this very question. Its visionary final report, *Learning: The treasure within*, identified four critical arenas of learning for human growth and development to face the challenges ahead:

- learning to be
- learning to know
- learning to do
- learning to live together

The report remains a fount of wisdom and insight. It has won powerful support and has nominally underpinned many education reform efforts around the world. None has yet fully realised the vision, however, still tending to pour this potent 21st-century wine into unsuitable 20th-century bottles.

The OECD took up the challenge in late 1997. Once again it brought together international researchers for an inquiry over several years, this time to identify the "key competencies for a successful life and a well-functioning society in the 21st century".

This inquiry too was deep and comprehensive, drawing on the best available wisdom from philosophers, sociologists, cognitive scientists and others and including consultations with all OECD member countries. It included a rigorous discussion of what might be meant by 'competence' in the world of the 21st century.

The authors started by sifting through lists of possible attributes needed to meet the goal of living a fulfilled life in a well-functioning society. Search the internet for 'thriving in the 21st century' today and you will find plenty of reports with dauntingly long lists.

The OECD search confirmed, as we have done, that in the operating conditions of the 21st century none of these competencies is of any use, nor can they be developed in practice, unless we can first become more adept at reading the landscape and finding our feet in complexity and uncertainty. The first step is awareness.

Further, they reached a powerful consensus that the only way to know whether the capacity to act effectively in complexity is present is to see it demonstrated in practice.

They arrived at a simple definition of 'competence' in the 21st century: "competence is the ability to meet important challenges in life in a complex world".

This is an important insight. It identifies competence not as an attainment but as a practice. It implies that you cannot measure or assess 21st-century competencies in the abstract. You can only see them demonstrated in action. They can be inferred from successful performance in complex situations in the real world.

It further suggests that they are also developed in practice. To return to the Federer example, you do not become a great tennis player by reading more books (although that can help) – you have to perform, try things out, learn through experience. It is the same with the 21st-century competencies.

We Are Already Competent

Human maturation is not a mechanical, linear development, but an emergent process achieved uniquely by each individual in their historical confrontation with the existential demands of their own life. It begins with an embodied potential – we are born to become – and unfolds uniquely, in each moment, with each choice.

The metaphor is organic. When we think of human development it should not be in terms of ladders, or levels, or software upgrades. We are talking about natural human processes of growth, discovery, expansion, transformation.

Donald Winnicott, the pioneering paediatrician and child psychiatrist, offered a beautifully simple formula in talking about child development. He saw the child like a seed or a bulb, planted into fertile soil and containing in itself everything needed for healthy growth and development. Growth, he said, is a natural, maturational process in a facilitating environment.

It follows that we have the potential to be growing all the time, revealing and developing our innate capacities. With greater self-awareness and reflection and with the right enabling conditions for our learning, we will naturally expand to meet the challenges in front of us.

This stance is itself somewhat counter-cultural in the competence development field. Those long lists and inventories betray a fundamentally neurotic response. They are almost compulsive attempts to deny the three emergencies, offering instead the comforting promise that everything will be manageable if we only develop these necessary skills.

Each new competence spawns a separate module in a degree course, a tailored workshop from a training provider, or a raft of self-help books and instructional videos. The effect is to add to our sense of overwhelm and inadequacy and further deepen the cultural crisis.

It is possible to start from a different perspective. We are born with the potential and aspiration to express our full humanness but require the right supporting environment for this to develop. Throughout our history as a species, humans have created settings that support this inherent desire to become all we can be.

In other words, the 21st-century competencies are innate. We come designed for a complex world. It is true that our socialisation processes can tend to prune away these natural capacities over time. At birth, for example, we are capable of learning any language, a capacity that wanes as we become socialised into just one or two. But it is still there.

Likewise, we may encounter discrimination, inequality, injustice, abuse, structural and systemic violence of different kinds that poison the environment for learning, fail to provide a facilitating environment and thwart our natural development. That is why we must pay attention to wider environments, structures and cultures as much as to persons. Yet still at a fundamental level, as human beings, we have all we need and can in time, together, triumph even in adversity.

This is the message of Vaclav Havel's influential prison essay 'The Power of the Powerless', for example, inviting us in the face of totalitarian oppression to walk tall, assert our human dignity and "live in truth".

Havel is drawing on a view of the 'human personality' as always whole and entire. Our needs are complex, fluid and dynamic. All possibilities are always present. Which will manifest is contingent on experience in the world. We each of us exist in an ever-shifting and exquisitely attuned engagement between our interior lives and the external universe and it is in this engagement that 'being' proceeds. There is always more to discover.

Enabling Growth and Development

The Core Stance

How can we support this natural process of growth? The challenges in our environment might naturally call our 21st-century competencies from us. But so too can people, groups and patterns of relationship. How might we more effectively facilitate and support the growth and development of ourselves and others?

Decades of research validate the person-centred approach of the psychologist Carl Rogers, who put his faith in the future and in human nature. He saw human beings as full of potential and fundamentally oriented toward the good.

His approach assumed that any group or individual person, if encountered and accompanied in their discomfort by a non-shaming other and discouraged from denying reality or collapsing into fantasy or worse, will self-right, self-regulate, find a way through.

Sooner or later a new pattern of coherence will emerge out of confusion and conflict. And it will be unique to the circumstance, the individual or the group. In the words of the poet Antonio Machado, "Wanderer, there is no path. The path is made by walking."

Technically, Rogers suggested that the approach involves being 'congruent' or real with the other person(s), offering 'unconditional positive regard' and 'empathic understanding', communicating faith in people's inherent capacity to grow, create and transform.

Our friend Charlie Miller, who received an OBE for services to hairdressing in the Queen's 2012 New Year's Honours List and has a string of salons across Edinburgh, revels in the story of having a person-centred therapist 'in his chair' as a client for many years. When he heard him talking about the Rogerian approach to enabling growth and the full expression of the human personality, Miller immediately realised it could apply equally to the relationship between stylist and client.

He reframed it in his own terms as the basis for training new recruits:

- Authenticity: be honest, only offer what you can genuinely deliver, walk the talk;
- Empathy: don't impose on the client, remember it is their hair and their choice;
- Non-invasive warmth: establish a warm relationship but don't get too familiar.

Katie Colombus' excellent book, *How to Listen*, drawing on the experience of the Samaritans, is laced through with these same principles. It includes this vivid image:

"One of the things that stood out for me in my training was being told to imagine someone who's having a hard time… as if they're sitting in a pit. What friends and family will do, with the best of intentions, is to try and help them out of the pit. But as Samaritans, what we do instead is get down into the pit and sit alongside them to explore with them what that feels like…. One of the fundamental principles… is the belief that everyone knows what's best for them[selves]."

Alicia Garza's memoir about Black Lives Matter, *The Purpose of Power*, offers a societal example. She describes her experience of building movements across boundaries to 'interrupt' existing patterns and historical prejudice and open a space for new patterns to emerge.

She too describes a listening practice – her early experience of mobilising community going from door to door in West Oakland:

> *"I learned how to really listen for what was underneath 'No, I don't think I can make it'… I spent countless hours in kitchens and living rooms, on crowded couches and porches, and in backyards. I learned how to engage other people in the slow process of changing the world."*

The message is clear. To support growth and development we need to meet people where they are and then provide a space for them to grow.

Equally, our effectiveness in nurturing such growth will depend crucially on what we view as possible for the human being or beings in front of us.

On this last point we follow the lead of the Brazilian philosopher Roberto Unger, who offers an expansive perspective. Unger describes himself as a 'radical pragmatist', grounding his knowledge in the one thing he can trust – his own experience.

But what is that experience? Like all of us, he is conscious of living in a decaying organism (as he puts it), a living, vulnerable human body that over time starts to wear out. Yet at the same time he – like all of us – also has an equally real, pragmatic, lived experience of a God-like, infinite imagination.

As a politician (he has served in the Brazilian government) he observes that our public institutions pay far more attention to the first aspect of his experience than the second. He insists that we should "revise the institutional organisation and the ideological assumptions of society" to pay attention to our infinite capacity. We can then enable "a larger life – a life of greater intensity, of greater scope, and of greater capability for the ordinary man and woman." This is a developmental stance – permeating relationships, culture and institutions.

Another stand-out example would be Dr Ludwig Guttmann, who in 1944 became the first Director of the spinal injuries centre at Stoke Mandeville Hospital. He entered a world in which soldiers crippled on the front line were regarded as being as good as dead, living out the rest of their short lives under sedation, waiting only to be moved to the mortuary. Based on the evidence on recovery at that time, this was a perfectly rational approach. The men even arrived at the centre in coffins.

But Guttmann refused to accept that narrow view. He sensed the humanity and the potential in these people, people just like himself. He thought sport would be a good way for them to build up physical strength and to restore some self-respect. He staged the first Stoke Mandeville Games in 1948, the year of the London Olympics. By 1952 there were more than 130 competitors from around the world and the event, the Paralympic Games, is still run to this day.

Guttman did not see corpses – he saw potential. Even as these men lay in their coffins, he saw a possibility to support their growth and transformation. Tellingly, their growing competence was expressed through action.

The Facilitating Environment

We understand that the 'facilitating environment' for growth and development that Winnicott talks about must include people with a certain regard for humanity and the potential in all of us, and the capacity to enter into a warm, trusting, Rogerian relationship with others.

Beyond that, what are the practicalities of establishing learning environments embodying these qualities? What does it require to create and to 'hold' such spaces in practice? And beyond these foundations, what else might be necessary to support the growth response to powerful times?

A natural place to look might be to our institutions of education and formal learning. Yet in practice, with some notable exceptions, most have been unable to absorb the lessons of the OECD study identifying 21st-century competence as a practice rather than an achievement. They have struggled to do justice to the Delors Commission report even when they have tried to do so.

Nor are such spaces routinely found now in the world of work, where we might expect to learn through practice, working with others, on the job. IFF's work with the public sector, the private sector, the third sector and the arts suggests that, in practice, opportunities for transformative growth at work are few and far between.

If anything, the opposite is the case. There is plenty of evidence that the way we live and work today is leaving us unsatisfied, unfulfilled, unhappy and in many cases suffering mental distress. There is a yearning for something more fulfilling.

Gallup's recent research on 'How Millennials Want To Work And Live' found that Millennials in the US "don't just work for a paycheck – they want a purpose", they "are not pursuing job satisfaction – they are pursuing development" and they "don't want bosses – they want coaches".

This is no surprise. It reflects a trend that has been growing over twenty years at least. The psychologist Ian Mitroff found in 2005 in a series of interviews conducted across the corporate world in the US that:

"First, people desperately want an opportunity to realise their potential as whole human beings, both on and off the job. Second they want to work for ethical organisations. Third, they want to do interesting work. And while making money certainly is important, at best it is a distant fourth goal for most people."

At all levels and in all sectors, people are looking for a more fulfilling, more wholesome and more developmental work experience. Not only for selfish reasons, but from an instinctive sense that the reductionist, instrumental alternative is a failing paradigm choking off the growth response across the board.

Part of the appeal of the non-profit or social sector, by contrast, has always been its 'expressive' value – the opportunity it gives people to express their values through their work. Yet even here, for decades, investment in personal growth and development has taken a back seat to the ever-present demands of delivery.

The pandemic has dramatically disrupted the working environment for many, shifting processes online, replacing 'the office' with remote working, forcing a new balance between work and home life. There have been benefits for some, including the loss of the daily commute. But those benefits are unevenly distributed, and there have been considerable downsides.

In one recent poll almost half of managers in the UK said they were afraid their employees would burnout, through social isolation, general worries about their families and loved ones and the state of the world, and the erosion of the boundary between their personal and professional lives.

Maintaining connection and feeling part of a larger, stable and supportive whole can help. But here again surveys suggest that the longer remote working goes on, the more employees struggle to connect to and really feel part of their organisation and its culture. And all these trends tend to be worse for younger generations.

There is clearly an urgent need to create and maintain more spaces for growth, development and learning and to make them as open and accessible as possible in response to today's emergencies. There is an abundant latent competence in humanity, which we need to develop – but equally increasing evidence that existing patterns of working and organising are instead putting people under barely tolerable strain and choking off more generative possibilities.

We need to move beyond denial before it's too late, to admit the diminishing returns from our existing systems of education, work and training and begin consciously and intentionally to invest in spaces supporting human growth and the transformative growth response.

Spaces for Growth

What Kinds of Space?

In establishing such spaces, there is no single blueprint to follow.

At one level, if this is simply about providing a supportive, non-judgemental, attentive space for another person then, as How to Listen claims, "anyone can do it". There are simple structures of 'peer support' based on active listening and noticing ("You don't seem yourself today, are you OK?") plus conversational micro-competencies for how to respond when people choose to open up.

That will help as a first response. It is equally important to include a cognitive component. It is often cognitive overload, not being able to make sense of the world, that generates stress and its emotional consequences.

A walk on the seashore is certainly therapeutic, but a few simple frameworks with which to make cognitive sense of our world are equally valuable. Arguably more so in a professional context where decision-making in conditions of uncertainty and ambiguity is the primary, day-to-day challenge. To address the existential emergency we also need to pay attention to the conceptual.

Some level of individual and shared competence to support each other in these ways will help to sustain a human system. But what else might be needed to encourage it to grow?

It helps to think here in terms of enabling conditions for growth, the 'facilitating environment', rather than tools and techniques. The development process is experiential, learning through practice. It is stimulated by an approach not a curriculum.

Learners need to find themselves in an artfully convened space: where they feel safe to experiment and explore; able to follow their own path – in the company of others; supported and invited to expand their awareness and their horizons but without being forced down a pre-determined path; open to discovery, challenge and surprise; rooted in life and its demands; able to explore the outer reaches of their imagination and vision – whilst still paying attention to the day job.

The following pages offer some thoughts on the qualities that need to be brought into play to satisfy these functions. They apply equally whether we are considering a physical or a virtual space – or, as is likely in the future, a creative blend of the two.

Safe (Enough) Space

The space for growth and development will be challenging at times, provocative, edgy and uncomfortable. A good adaptive learning space generates enough anxiety to loosen certainties but will also feel safe enough to take a risk, to admit vulnerability, to explore new worldviews and so on.

Some get impatient with this concern for 'safety' and ask instead for 'brave' spaces where uncomfortable truths can be named and reality engaged. Yet even then, if they are not to be manipulative or oppressive, such spaces will need to operate from a ground of safety. As noted already in discussing the core stance (see page 26), transformative growth requires support.

Laura Pereira and other researchers working to establish 'transformative spaces' for this kind of learning in the global South have come up with the notion of 'safe enough' spaces to strike this balance. Such spaces are sensitive to issues of privilege and/or social oppression and tensions in the specific social context, but not so 'safe' that nothing happens.

The baseline is that we need to feel psychologically safe, that we are in good hands. Otherwise challenge will trigger defensive anxiety rather than learning.

We each vary a lot in what gives us a sense of security, but we can at least attend to the basics – physical, intellectual, emotional and social.

The physical dimension is most obvious, and also highlights the importance of the physical boundary – a delineation of 'our' space that others do not invade without notice. It should be obvious where the perimeter sits and how it is maintained.

The intellectual aspect can either provide baseline security for exploration or add to a sense of confusion and overwhelm. Be mindful of people's understanding of what is going on. Provide a conceptual framework that is reliable for making sense of events with some acceptable degree of uncertainty. Develop shared language, symbols and metaphors. Feed a common awareness of what is uncertain inherently and what could be clarified with more information.

Pay attention to the emotional landscape. Every thought expressed comes with a feeling. A psychologically safe space is one in which participants become aware of their feelings and are able to bring them into the space, express them, on their own terms.

The social dimensions of persons gathering in groups are legion and mostly unconscious. Here too the primary aim should be to create a space that can bring them to conscious awareness and also make them discussable. Appropriate use of ritual can be helpful. Opening with a silence, celebrating birthdays, naming gratitude at missions accomplished – all this creates a sense of collective membership that adds to psychological safety.

Some of these features might be brought about through technique and physical practices. Others are 'held' in the relationships between people

– qualities of being and presence rather than doing. Much of the work in creating and maintaining a safe enough space will be subtle and almost invisible, but with attention it is an art that can be learned.

Empty space

A space prepared for safety subsequently becomes populated with people. Anything is now possible. The human drama can unfold and magic can happen. This is where we can learn a great deal from the world of theatre. The director Peter Brook's classic volume of essays *The Empty Space* provides an excellent sourcebook.

> *"I can take any empty space and call it a bare stage", he writes. "A man walks across this empty space while someone else is watching him, and this is all that is needed for an act of theatre to be engaged."*

This is the essence of human interaction. It is also the essence of reflective practice. Between them the actor and the observer have created a space out of nothing, a human space that can now move and expand and enable in any direction.

Keith Johnstone's excellent book on improvisation starts from the same simple framework – two persons interacting in an empty space – from which whole worlds can be imagined into being.

Brook's essays beautifully describe the space created and held between actors and audience, which can on occasion transform the base material of ordinary and familiar exchange into something freighted with meaning, "in which each moment is lived more clearly and more tensely". The mundane is revealed in a new light, we see into the inner life. There is a moment of insight, of transformation.

The effect is created mutually – it lives in the space between actor and audience. As we would expect when the Rogerian principles are honoured, the quality of the audience's listening and attention raises the quality of the actors' performance – there are good houses and bad houses. If we are 'holding' space for others it is the quality of our attention to that space that will make it potentially transformative.

This is less about doing and more about being, particularly knowing intuitively how long you dare hold the moment without intervention. Brook describes a production of *Measure for Measure* in which the empty space is filled with silence:

> *"I asked Isabella, before kneeling for Angelo's life, to pause each night until she felt the audience could take it no longer – and this used to lead to a two-minute stopping of the play. The device became a voodoo pole – a silence in which all the invisible elements of the evening came together, a silence in which the abstract notion of mercy became concrete for that moment to those present."*

He is eloquent on the role of the director, who is "there to attack and yield, provoke and withdraw, until the indefinable stuff begins to flow." As already noted, the space must be safe, but within it we need to be brave. That applies as much to the guide as to the participants.

There is no easy blueprint, no linear method, no plan. "In a sense the director is always an imposter, a guide at night who does not know the territory, and yet has no choice – he must guide, learning the route as he goes."

The theatre is living and immediate. "A director learns that the growth of rehearsals is a developing process; he sees that there is a right time for everything, and his art is the art of recognising these moments." These are literacies. The first step is awareness.

In thinking about learning and development we are not generally trying to coax a performance out of a troupe of actors. But we may be trying to encourage persons to find a character in themselves, an expansion of their day-to-day capacity, new ways of interacting with or responding to others, something that lies just beyond their learning edge.

What Brook teaches us – alongside some simple exercises for exploring the miracle of human-to-human communication – is the subtle role of direction in these processes, and the crucial role of everybody in the room in creating the space. Listening grants speaking. We pay attention, like a gift.

Reflective Space

The capacity for self-awareness and reflection is a 'threshold competence', one that opens up the route to developing other attributes, the key to the treasure within. Harold Bridger described this as 'the double task' – to be able to act and reflect on one's actions at the same time. It is the beginning of wisdom.

The space for growth and development needs to encourage this quality. Therapists are sometimes trained to imagine another version of themselves sitting in the top corner of the room, up against the ceiling, looking down on them as they perform. We can cultivate the same habit in ourselves.

Mindfulness exercises and periods of shared silence can help. Eugene Gendlin's 'focusing' technique helps participants become grounded in a space, aware of themselves and fully present to the ongoing flow of experience. That opens up channels of perception and self-awareness. There is a ritual element too in such shared practices which, as noted previously, can help a group become more aware of itself.

Given that we believe the 21st-century competencies are innate, the critical process of growth involves offering people an experience that engages them in some activity and then an opportunity to reflect on it. In this way, even in simple shared exercises and experiences they will discover things about themselves and about the pattern of relationships they find themselves in. Doing this in a group process encourages a diversity of perspectives, multiple ways of knowing and processing a common experience – which accelerates the learning.

This is an approach at odds with the traditional passing on of technical tools or methods, or abstract information. But it is what is required of those professionals likely to be most effective in dealing with complexity and uncertainty in the real world.

The challenge today is to make sense of each set of unique circumstances as we go, drawing on reserves of experience, intuition, tacit knowledge and all the hidden skills and capacities that technical rationality has relegated to obscurity. This is a learning stance of reflection in action, an art more than a science.

Indeed, the arts – dance, movement, making, music, poetry and so on – can play an important part in opening new channels of perception and reflection. The space we create will be poorer without them. In particular, they can allow what we might call 'the transcendent' to enter the room – a spiritual dimension, a spirit, that informs all of our lives but that we have become reluctant to acknowledge in public.

Expansive Space

The space needs to be expansive, to provide room for, and to provoke growth and development in, people's knowing, being and understanding. As noted previously, overwhelm is not just emotional, it is cognitive as well. Some help in coming to terms with the conceptual emergency will have a beneficial impact on the existential emergency that is inevitably part of transformative learning.

IFF has articulated five critical shifts that can help to enhance our range and understanding in powerful times, moving beyond a traditional Western Enlightenment worldview. Encouraging and being open to these shifts in perspective will expand the cognitive range of any space in which they are incorporated and honoured.

From Subject-Object to Subject-Subject: Many of the triumphs of Enlightenment thinking came from taking the objective viewpoint, separating an observer who is conscious and aware from the thing observed, which is assumed not to be. That is a partial view. It needs to be complemented by a worldview that sees ourselves as subjects and participants – a relational universe.

This is why Carl Rogers insists on the concept of the 'person' rather than the 'individual'. A person exists only in relationship, living a life within a pattern of other lives. Likewise, there are qualities of life, like love and language, that can only be held in common. When we meet subject to subject, whether with another person, a tree or an ocean, the encounter changes both and a new universe unfolds.

The triumphs of Enlightenment reason came from suppressing this subject-subject worldview. Think of it as 'second order cybernetics': the difference between phoning home to say you are stuck in traffic and phoning to say that you are traffic.

Expand What Constitutes Valid Knowledge: We tend to honour and privilege a small subset of human knowledge based on abstract rationalism. It is the basis of our science, public policy, management, education. It has also provided the justification for ignoring and invalidating the knowledge of marginalised persons throughout history. In a complex world we need to expand our worldview to include also 'non-rational' knowledge as found in the arts, in music, in intuition, in acts of the imagination, in embodied knowledge, in the science of qualities as much as the science of quantities.

We should also reclaim and value collective knowledge that emerges in groups, knowledge that arises out of being in relationship (no one is as intelligent as everyone), knowledge that rests in communities, indigenous knowledge. All knowledge is local, contextual, the product of a culture. In

the West we have elevated some forms of knowing over others – see the syllabus at our elite universities. But we need to admit a broader range of knowledge if we are going to make effective decisions in today's world.

From Organisation to Integrity: This shift is based on the work of Martin Albrow and his observation that what we call an 'organisation' today is in practice a dynamic pattern of relationships between its own members and between them and an ever-changing world of competing loyalties and different value systems. It is a human system, a 'human being'. Albrow calls this an 'integrity' – an organisational form that maintains a collective moral purpose over time and is therefore willing to be held responsible for its actions even in an uncertain world.

Individuals will belong to many different integrities: organisations, political parties, social clubs, religious denominations, the family and so on. Each negotiates its relationship with the world around the four poles of recognition, sovereignty, reciprocity and agency. The integrity model has proven to be a useful diagnostic for groups and teams – to help them work together, to work with others, and to identify and maintain their own integrity.

Shift in Our Relationship With Time: It is a defining characteristic of Enlightenment thought to make time a measurable and therefore a scarce resource. Some cultures see time as infinite rather than scarce and cyclical rather than linear. In the West we tend to regard natural resources as infinite and time as limited when in reality it is the other way round. This shift encourages us to see and to manage a world of flows rather than stocks. What may look like a fixed structure is revealed as slow-moving process. Everything flows – but at different rates.

The cyclical view of time helps to shift our sense of an ending, which is always an echo of our fear of death. We need to complete, to close well and with grace – understanding that this is what makes room for the next cycle. An expansive perspective pays attention to endings as much as beginnings, hospice work for the dying culture alomgside midwifery for the new.

From Fragmentation to Wholeness: The Enlightenment perspective is reductive, breaking complex systems down into discrete parts in order to understand them. An expansive perspective favours holism, connection, integration and a systemic view. These are not alternatives but complementary: the ideal is 'holism with focus'.

Ultimately the whole is contained in the part, and vice versa. William Blake claimed to be able to see the world in a grain of sand. We are artists of our own lives, in a pattern of relationship with other lives. We must always be paying attention to our needs as an individual to survive, but equally cannot be healthy alone. This is an inevitable tension – 'being me and also us' – which cannot be denied.

An expansive space will encourage and honour these five invitations to move beyond an Enlightenment consciousness.

Liminal Space

A space for development, from which one emerges somehow transformed and subtly changed, has an element of magic and mystery about it. It is a 'liminal space' – the space between, a limbo, neither the new world nor the old. It is a temporary space, like the enchanted forest or a dream, from which we expect to return.

The Latin root is 'limen' meaning threshold. We cross a threshold into a liminal space, and we do not recognise the territory we find there. It is a land of mystery, uneasiness and discovery.

In some ways, the existential emergency stems from just such a condition. In powerful times we have lost faith in the old rules and patterns but not yet found new ones. Gramsci wrote that in this gap "a great variety of morbid symptoms appear". But equally this can be an opening to learning, growth and expansion.

In a liminal space, between structures, we can be held in our confusion long enough for new patterns of coherence to form. We need a space in which to acknowledge the crisis, the unknowing and to stay with it. Transformative growth will not come from giving in to the impulse to settle for quick fixes or one of the ever ready 'ten steps to wellbeing' programmes. Rather, look for the creative edge: where we feel something's brewing that could take us to a new resolution.

People's psychological defence mechanisms serve a purpose and we must respect that. There is trepidation in stepping into the dark wood. But eventually breakthroughs occur. They are not engineered. They are transforming moments, self-organising, spontaneous. The moment the future becomes present.

The standard metaphor for transformative change is the process by which a caterpillar turns into a butterfly. This is indeed remarkable. The caterpillar weaves itself a cocoon, then effectively dissolves itself into a kind of soup. That soup includes 'imaginal cells' which endure the dissolution to act as the foundational structure to reconfigure the rest of the material into a butterfly.

It is an alluring metaphor for human development – the imaginal cells containing a presentiment of the future. But human development is different and altogether more alchemical. We know that a caterpillar will turn into a butterfly, and indeed what kind of butterfly. But human transformation, individual and collective, is utterly unpredictable. It can happen at any time. And we do not know what will result until it has resulted.

It is imagination, enchantment and surprise that characterise human transformation, not biological process. Coleridge wrote of "the willing suspension of disbelief" that allows us to immerse ourselves in alternative realities for a while. Keats praised a quality of 'Negative Capability' – "when man is capable of being in uncertainties, mysteries, doubts, without any irritable reaching after fact and reason."

By keeping this in mind we can consciously design spaces that are not just revealing of life, not just facilitative of growth, but capable of enticing us into a parallel alternate realm affording deep insight and unexpected change.

In the next section we encounter the creative practice of Helen Marriage, a producer of such spaces on the grand scale. Like bringing a giant puppet show, 'The Sultan's Elephant', to the streets of London over four days in May 2006. There is footage of David Lammy MP, then Minister of Culture, standing on the steps of the National Gallery in Trafalgar Square addressing the weekend crowd, exulting in the collective rediscovery of belief in "joy, wonder and magic". They had been drawn into enchantment.

Marriage's practice, often working with the power of myth and fairy story – familiar sources of other-worldly transformation – involves the public creation of liminal space. It is magic manifesting in real life on a city-wide scale. She introduces a temporary disruption to normal patterns, familiar landscapes. The city becomes a stage. It flexes to accommodate the artistic project and performance. Audience, actors, administrators, city officials, bureaucrats, everyone involved has a part in creating and sustaining the magic.

Once the show is over, everything must return to normal, as if it had never happened. That is part of what makes it liminal and transformative – was that real, or was it all a dream? The streets once again become an 'empty space'. But the space itself is transformed. It is not possible to walk those same streets now as previously. They have revealed their hidden potential and will forever ovoke it in those who were there to see it.

There is a read-across here to Hakim Bey's notion of 'Temporary Autonomous Zones', deliberately created at the boundaries of established patterns to provide spaces to escape formal structures of control. 'Burning Man', a temporary city/festival erected in the Nevada desert every year and now with a hundred regional chapters around the world, is the best-known example. These structures are designed to be temporary and are dismantled after use, on the assumption that anything permanent would deteriorate into formality and lose its creative spirit.

Carl Rogers used this idea to help groups resolve seemingly intractable divisions. His invention of the encounter group in the late 1960s created liminal spaces in which people on different sides of conflict could engage their differences to meet as persons and find ways to mutual respect. Gender, race, sexuality, violence, the war in Vietnam, the 'troubles' in Northern Ireland – issues that otherwise seemed too hot to handle – could be explored within the safety of temporary spaces, expertly held.

At a personal level, IFF uses a framework called 'Power and Edge' developed by our late friend and colleague Jim Ewing. It suggests that we all have certain go-to competencies, techniques, talents, capacities that we know we can rely on – our 'power'. These feel reliable and permanent. At the same time we also have other capacities, less developed perhaps, less conscious, but there all the same – our edge. Others can often see our 'edge' more clearly than we can ("That time you drew a cartoon for the report, you should do it more often. You're really good at it.").

Especially when we are in a crisis or under pressure, we tend to fall back on our power. In order to develop our edge, we need consciously to put our power to one side, to try something else. We need to step across the threshold, into more risky territory. Dancing at the edge.

We are more likely to do so, to expand and grow into our innate capacities, if we are in a safe enough space, a reflective space for rehearsal and discovery, an empty space full of potential, an expansive space inviting us to try on other worldviews for size, and a liminal space – which we understand as temporary, through which we pass, and from which we can and will return.

Prophetic Space

Last on this short list of the qualities of different kinds of space is prophetic space. It comes last not because it is least. This is perhaps the most powerful kind of space and the most elusive.

The concept draws on the thinking of Walter Brueggemann, an old testament scholar who has written widely on the role of the prophet in society. He identifies the work of what he calls "the prophetic imagination… to walk our society into the crisis where it does not want to go, and to walk our society out of that crisis into newness that it does not believe is possible". This is a rare, liminal, capacity – to hold people between two worlds, between hope and despair.

In *Reality, Grief, Hope: Three urgent prophetic tasks* Brueggemann explores the enabling conditions for this quality of prophetic imagination to be expressed, especially in moments of crisis.

First, we must embrace the reality of what has occurred and what is revealed. He speaks of facing up to reality where it might clash with official ideology. Then we can acknowledge our pain and grieve for what is lost: grief in the midst of denial. Only after such preparation can we fashion an authentic hope, a mature hope that is not fantasy or escapism, a hope that engages with reality, a hope that speaks to and springs from our moral core.

Brueggemann's inquiry concerns how to restore the church as a space in which the prophetic voice might be heard. For the voice of prophecy is drawn from us by the 'space' we find ourselves in. It arises, he says, "in a way that contradicts the evident facts on the ground, contradicts what the listener expected to hear, and contradicts what the speaker intended to say". It comes "from elsewhere".

Brueggemann highlights Martin Luther King Jr's "I have a dream" speech as the voice of prophetic imagination. "What King does is fill the space in the liminal season of US life between old failed racism and new human community with the cadences of possibility." We might also have heard this voice at the Inauguration of President Biden in January 2021 in the stirring words of a young poet, Amanda Gorman, who proclaimed that America is not broken just unfinished.

What kind of a space can bring forth this voice? Brueggemann calls on us to nurture spaces of imagination "in which unuttered possibility is uttered, thoughts beyond our thoughts are thought, and ways beyond our ways are known". This is the highest bar – but consistent with all that has gone before.

Hosts and Guides

To conclude this section, it is worth taking a moment to think about two important roles required for all of these spaces: hosts and guides.

Hosting is about establishing a space, inviting people into it and looking after them when they are there. Where the purpose of such spaces is learning, growth and development it also helps to have a guide, like Peter Brook, to accompany the participants on a journey into and through the unknown and to help them find the meaning in their experience.

There is a vast storehouse of resources for anyone wishing to host generative gatherings, many written during the heyday of personal growth workshops which began in California in the 1960s and spread around the globe allowing an entire generation to push themselves to their liminal edge.

Priya Parker offers a rich and valuable contemporary guide in her *The Art of Gathering*. She is particularly good on openings and endings, the liminal, threshold-crossing moments for a group or a gathering that effectively frame and create a space. She observes, for example, that the space opens as soon as the invitation is issued.

On hosting itself, she identifies the need for somebody to exercise 'generous authority' – in other words to hold authority in service of the group. The host's role is to protect the guests (ensure a safe space), to equalise the guests (have them participate as equals) and to connect the guests (perform introductions, turn the individuals into a group).

She suggests that we can rely on 'etiquette' for a cohesive group that has absorbed a common culture, where the 'rules' of behaviour can remain unwritten. Otherwise we need Rules, which help to establish 'a temporary world'. Rules rather than etiquette allow for greater diversity. And the expressed purpose of the gathering, the purpose of establishing the space, should act as the bouncer on the door. Though not always possible to prevent, persons who do not share the purpose of the gathering should not be admitted to the space.

To act as a guide in these spaces, into and through the territory of growth, development and possibility, can be challenging and is more an art than a science. Dante chose the poet Virgil to guide him through purgatory (another liminal space) in his *Divine Comedy* and the female presence of Beatrice to complete the journey through Heaven.

Gerard Egan, whose *The Skilled Helper* offers what has become a widely used approach to person-centred counselling, likewise suggests that a certain degree of worldly wisdom, an expertise in "the fundamental pragmatics of life", is required to be a confident and competent guide.

Carl Rogers offered his own thoughts on the role in an essay from 1969. He outlines a number of propositions which resonate nicely with the qualities of space already discussed.

Guides, he suggests, should make available the widest possible range of opportunities for learning – including themselves as a resource for the group. They should be alive to both the intellectual content and the emotional feelings expressed, or not expressed, in the group, being particularly alert for anything indicative of deep or strong feelings.

Once the tone and climate of the group is established, Rogers suggests that the guide can increasingly become "a participant learner, a member of the group". Throughout, as a facilitator of learning, the guide "endeavours to recognise and accept his or her own limitations".

The takeaway message, just as in Peter Brook's essays, is that the guide is in the process, not just managing it. Audience and actor are one, co-creating an experience from which they both learn and through which they might both be transformed.

Section Three:
Transformative Action

Moving Into Action

Producing

If the first step towards becoming comfortable and effective in today's operating environment is awareness, and the second is growth, the third – the proof of the pudding – is transformative action.

Sooner or later our 21st-century competencies must be demonstrated and developed in action. As one of the pioneers of action learning, Reg Revans, wrote, "there can be no learning without action, and no action without learning." We have found our feet, grown our competencies, now we must act – "meeting important challenges in life in a complex world".

We will inevitably be working with others (we cannot be competent alone). We will want to convene together in ways that honour what has already been discussed, designed to bring the best out of ourselves and our relationships.

But what kind of action? In the service of growth and transformation, our actions will disappoint if they are simply expressions of a neurotic defence that denies reality (one more heave) or of psychotic hysteria, high on excitement and confusion (the logic of 'disruption', move fast and break things).

We will be looking for a transformative growth response, working with the life force, configuring new sources of abundance.

We have written extensively elsewhere about this as a practice of 'transformative innovation', grounded in practical hope. Here we concentrate on the human aspects of that practice, the people.

This work will call upon a different set of skills – not hosting or guiding but producing. It is a role championed by Roanne Dods, who led ground-breaking work on the producer role in the realm of the arts during her time heading the Jerwood Charitable Foundation.

She saw that the arts are not just about artists and 'arts organisations'. There are also certain individuals who have the skill and capacity to mediate between creative artists on the one hand and structures of funding and accountability on the other to deliver acts of the imagination that are (by definition) unique and original.

This same underlying challenge also describes the practice of transformative innovation and the exercise of 21st-century competence. We need to bring diverse talents together across boundaries, bring imaginative ideas to life, whilst all the time being highly aware of the cultural and psychological context and the challenge of introducing the new in the presence of the old.

The best source book is Kate Tyndall's *The Producers: Alchemists of the Impossible*. It offers a series of rich interviews with arts producers in many disciplines and gives a flavour of the role and the activities involved.

As noted in the previous section on liminal spaces, we have found it particularly useful to study the example of Helen Marriage. What does she do to bridge the gap between insight and action, to move our competencies into effective, transformative practice? The essence of the approach can be summarised in the following seven practices.

Don't start from "this is impossible". That is self-defeating. As a producer you must believe that what you are proposing is possible. What drives the system is belief.

There are no rules (even where there are rules). The producer is not reckless and operates from a ground of care and responsibility. But they are also aware that following 'the rules' will generate only the familiar. Start with an intention and configure the necessary rules around that.

Get the fears articulated. This is a corollary to flexing the rule book. If we do that, people will be anxious. The rules are there as a defence: when it is taken away people will feel vulnerable. It is important therefore to understand those anxieties and to deal with them responsibly. When they form part of the conversation, and part of the design, when they are fully acknowledged, it provides comfort and reassurance, and enables participants to move into creative action.

Make friends. Marriage exemplifies the insight that whatever else we are dealing with, when it comes to getting anything done we are operating in a human system. The fears that are articulated are personal, owned by individuals, expressed as subjective emotion. Like Rogers, the rapport she establishes lives at a human level, not only in technical risk management reports and scenario planning. Transformative work is personal.

Take responsibility and seek contribution. The flip side of risk is responsibility. This comes across as Marriage's primary role as producer, the step that reveals and liberates resources: taking responsibility. Somebody has to do this. It provides comfort to the group and a point of stability around which rich resources can configure. Here she takes on a role we discussed earlier, as guide or director, giving people confidence to follow her into new territory. It is as unfamiliar to her as to others, but she has the courage and experience that comes from having crossed many such thresholds before. And an unshakeable faith in human nature and human capacity.

Don't ask for permission – it cannot be given. In moving into unknown territory, it is difficult for institutions to give permission to go ahead with something that is both unprecedented and beyond their individual domain of control. Marriage pre-empts the question: "the buck stops with me".

Push the ambition. The temptation is always to compromise in order to get things done. Something is better than nothing – right? That kind of thinking flashes warning lights to anyone seeking the transformative growth response. Compromise will be necessary at times. But the creative producer must start from the principle that anything is possible. If we are bold enough the world will flex to accommodate our ambition and all those involved will grow in delivering it.

A Culture of Transformation

Marriage's work is also illuminating in that, as previously discussed, it is explicitly about cultural disruption and transformation. Her role is not simply to bring a set of competencies, qualities, tools, techniques and experience to a situation (although she does all of that). She also carries a culture with her. Part of the impact of what she does – and one of the clues to its longer-term effects – lies in implanting a little of that culture wherever she goes.

This is not unusual: we all do it. Every intervention is a cultural intervention in that it carries an often unacknowledged and invisible set of behavioural norms, references, history and worldview with it. The difference is that Marriage is conscious of this. She has a high degree of cultural literacy. She knows that how she gets things done is as important as what gets done. Means and ends are one.

We see in the cultural pattern she embodies a number of distinctive characteristics to bear in mind as we move into transformative action. We are not only getting things done, we are also creating culture as we do so. Let's pay attention.

The culture is respectful. As noted throughout, it matters how we view the human beings in front of us. Deep and genuine respect for others is important, avoiding arbitrary exclusion. Such respect helps the producer work authentically with others, able to see things genuinely from their point of view, to walk in their shoes, to own their anxieties and challenges as if they were their own. It is easy to write others off as obstructive or bureaucratic or timeserving or simply not up to the task ("they just don't get it"). But that is incompatible with a creative culture of 'joy, wonder and magic' that draws the best from all involved.

The culture is trusting. If we are to draw the best from people, we must trust not only that it is there but that it will show itself if the circumstances are right. 'The Sultan's Elephant', for example, progressed with minimal crowd control, minimal attention to health and safety regulations, minimal infrastructure for such a huge public gathering. Part of the culture it embodied was to trust people to behave well, to look after themselves and each other and not to do anything stupid. When we operate from those principles people rise to them – but how often are we given the chance to show that side of our nature?

The culture is responsible. At one level this seems trivial: producers produce and so the culture is one of delivery. This is a culture that gets things done. That is related to the culture of trust: in order to engender trust you have to be trustworthy, and that means you must be open about what you can and cannot deliver, and reliable in the commitments you make. When Marriage says that something can be done it is not a rhetorical device: she means it. She takes responsibility for the things nobody else can handle, and in doing so encourages others to take responsibility in their own domains. She keeps her promises, however challenging they might turn out to be. That is a powerful injection into any culture.

But there is also a deeper sense of responsibility that is needed – a culture of care for those involved in the process. Do not push people too far, ask them for things they cannot do, add to their anxiety. The same applies to the producer. All of that fear, anxiety and worry has to be held somewhere – and the producer ends up holding much of it. It helps to have a buddy, a mentor, a supervisor. We all need somebody else on the end of the rope: no solo climbers.

The culture is meticulous. This is very striking and of a piece with the importance of trust and responsibility. Planning and attention to detail needs to be rigorous and applies as much to the web of human relationships as it does to material things – no stone is left unturned, nothing is too much trouble. The phrase 'nothing is left to chance' comes to mind as capturing the detailed nature of this kind of work.

Except that the point of all this preparation is precisely to allow for 'chance' to play as great a role as possible. The producer pays meticulous attention, in other words, to the enabling conditions rather than to controlling the event. There is thorough preparation but no rehearsal. That stance maximises the transformative impact.

The culture demands quality. We can be moved by scale – the spectacular, the blockbuster. But transformation occurs in the more mysterious realm where the science of qualities is in play. "Quality is essential", says Marriage. She trusts people to detect in an instant the difference, the cutting of corners, the shoddy compromise, the artifice, the lack of attention to detail that might break the spell, destroy the magic.

The culture promotes freedom. The producer provides just enough structure for life to reveal itself. And life is full of surprises, wonderfully abundant and free. The producer, as host and guide, names a time, a place, a number of artistic collaborators and then takes responsibility for making something happen. These simple moves create an otherwise unfettered space for contribution. With the right kind of attention, minimal structure coupled with maximum ambition frees up people and resources to behave differently, to contribute in novel ways in a new context.

The culture feeds hope. This too is explicit and all-pervading. Part of the creative producer's stance in the world is that anything is possible. The experiences they create are intended to awaken that feeling in those who participate in them – or even just hear about them. That feeling once experienced is never forgotten and can be called upon again and again. It is transformative.

The way to shift a culture is through conscious cultural intervention. Small acts of creative transgression that carry a culture with them.

We can see the same essential practice manifest in other areas – particularly in the public and social sectors where this accurately describes the practice of transformative innovation.

Patterns of novel practice, underpinned by a strong set of values, can usually be traced back to a committed champion. That champion has used her producer competencies to configure diverse people and resources into a viable operating pattern, the demonstration at a small scale of a new culture, getting something new and inspirational off the ground. This is a manifestation of the transformative growth response.

The First Move

Start Where You Are

If you have read this far you likely agree that creating and maintaining spaces and practices to help everybody develop their innate ability to flourish in the 21st century, and then to demonstrate their competencies in transformative, creative action, is both an urgent and a vital task. You may also feel that it is a daunting one.

It does not have to be complicated. Our best advice is to start where you are, with those around you. Just as the 21st-century competencies are innate, so too is the capacity to provide the 'facilitating environment' to enable their development in others.

We can take an initiative at any moment. In a world of flows, once we decide to take action we have already started. We maintain or disrupt the wider patterns in the culture through our participation in them. As living beings we are always growing and always inevitably intervening in the culture. Always responding and always influencing.

It would be good to establish and maintain scores of spaces with all the characteristics discussed in this booklet, hosted with grace and guided with the subtlety of a master.

At the same time, that will never be enough. The challenge is pervasive: we all need to find the facilitating environment, the enabling conditions, to help us flourish in today's world. The Appendix offers a few simple, intuitive tools and frameworks that can bring this approach to human growth and development into any setting, any conversation, any group, any relationship. Street-level practice.

The advice then is to find a friend and get started. Take inspiration from George Saunders, the award-winning writer of short stories – beautifully crafted, liminal, temporary worlds. A short story does not start with an idea, or a programme, or a plot, or a plan he says...

..."It starts with a sentence."

Appendix/Notes

IFF Resources

The themes and ideas in this booklet are explored in greater detail in a number of other IFF books and publications as follows:

- *Dancing at the Edge: Competence, culture and organisation in the 21st century*;
- *Transformative Innovation: A guide to practice and policy for system transition*;
- *Ten Things to do in a Conceptual Emergency*;
- *Cultivating a Culture of Kindness: A brief guide to peer support in the workplace*;
- *The Producer Role and the Art of the Impossible*.

In addition, IFF has developed two simple resources, a deck of prompt cards and a mini-Kitbag, to help initiate and create the kinds of space described in this booklet, artefacts to encourage the essentials of the transformative growth response to carry in your pocket (even if all you have in your pocket is your phone).

The prompt cards are a collection of statements derived from IFF's practical work, each inviting a shift out of familiar patterns of being, perceiving, thinking, framing towards something more expansive and capacious. They are about learning, direction, integrity, perception – "Recognise the different value patterns", "Perception first, then analysis", "Tolerate differences in order to discover richer wholeness" and so on. They are particularly good for encouraging the shifts described earlier in the section on a 'second enlightenment' frame (page 38). Many of them also naturally prompt the core producer competencies.

The prompts are designed as a deck of cards to make them easy and fun to use in very accessible ways. They lend themselves to all kinds of games: there is a particularly popular 'tarot' reading, and a game called 'strategy poker'. Above all each one offers a simple reminder – a timely prompt – of ways of knowing, being, doing and being together that we already possess but need to be encouraged to bring to the surface.

Kitbag grew from the same roots as IFF's wider work on competence in complexity and particularly the possible impacts on mental health and resilience of living 'in over our heads'. It helps in particular in developing psychological literacy, the ability to own our psychological responses to being stressed, troubled or overwhelmed, rather than becoming a victim of them.

The mini-Kitbag contains four simple resources – some short exercises to still the mind, a one-minute egg-timer, a feelings card offering a palette of different colours, and a set of animal cards representing different positive human qualities (trust, power, love, understanding, hope, etc.).

They can be introduced lightly and playfully into any setting, usually a small group, and will encourage people to become calm and settled, sharing feelings, encouraging reflection, opening up dialogue, growing mutual understanding and inspiring hope.

These are just two examples of simple, entry-level resources and 'micro-competencies' that can help ease us into this vital work. Towards the other end of the spectrum is IFF's Competence in Complexity programme, a year-long process embracing all three steps – awareness, growth and action – outlined in this booklet.

References
Besides various IFF resources and publications, several other published sources are referenced throughout this booklet. In some cases the text identifies both the author and the referenced work in question. What follows is a list of references where the author alone is referred to in the text. They are gathered here in the order in which they appear in the text and may be treated as 'further reading'.

Eamonn Kelly (2005) *Powerful Times: Rising to the challenge of our uncertain world*, Pearson Prentice Hall

Iona Heath (2012) *Love's Labours Lost: Why society is straitjacketing its professionals and how we might release them*, IFF Scotland

Charles Perrow (1999) *Normal Accidents: Living with high risk technologies*, Princeton University Press

Delors, J., Al Mufti, I., Amagi, I., Carneiro, R., Chung, F. *et al.* (1996) *Learning: The treasure within. Report to UNESCO of the International Commission on Education for the Twenty-First Century.* UNESCO Publishing

OECD (Organization for Economic Co-operation and Development) (2003) *Key Competencies for a Successful Life and a Well-Functioning Society* (ed. Rychen D.S. & Salganik L.H.), Hogrefe & Huber

Vaclav Havel (1978) 'The Power of the Powerless' in *Open Letters: Selected writings: 1965-1990*, edited and translated by Paul Wilson, Random House

Carl R. Rogers (1961) *On Becoming a Person*, Houghton Mifflin Company

Katie Colombus (2021) *How to Listen: Tools for opening up conversations when it matters most*, Samaritans

Alicia Garza (2020) *The Purpose of Power: How to build movements for the 21st century*, Doubleday

Roberto Unger (2009) *The Self Awakened: Pragmatism unbound*, Harvard University Press

Gallup (2021) *How Millennials Want to Live and Work*

Ian Mitroff (2005) *Why Some Companies Emerge Stronger and Better from a Crisis: Seven essential lessons for surviving disaster*, American Management Association

Dominic Brown (2021) 'Millennials and Covid-19: The unlucky generation' in *The Edge* magazine Vol 5, Cushman & Wakefield

Pereira, L., Frantzeskaki, N., Hebinck, A. *et al.* 'Transformative Spaces in the Making: Key lessons from nine cases in the Global South' in *Sustainability Science* 15, 61–178, Springer

Peter Brook (1969) *The Empty Space*, Discus Books

Keith Johnstone (1979) *Impro: Improvisation and the theatre*, Faber and Faber

Harold Bridger (1990) `Courses and Working Conferences as Transitional Learning Institutions', in E. Trist and H. Murray (eds) *The Social Engagement of Social Science*, Vol. 1., University of Pennsylvania Press

Eugene Gendlin (1978) *Focusing*, Everest House

Allison Stallibrass (1989) *Being Me and Also Us: Lessons from the Peckham experiment*, Scottish Academic Press

Artichoke (2006) *The Sultan's Elephant* - www.artichoke.uk.com/project/the-sultans-elephant/

Hakim Bey (1991) *TAZ: the Temporary Autonomous Zone*, Pacific Publishing Studio

Carl R Rogers (1957) 'Personal Thoughts on Teaching and Learning' in *Merrill Palmer Quarterly*, Vol 3 No 4, Wayne State University Press

George Saunders (2021) *A Swim in a Pond in the Rain,* Bloomsbury

About the Authors

Maureen O'Hara PhD is Professor of Psychology, National University, USA; President Emerita, Saybrook University, San Francisco; and Director, International Futures Forum-US. She is a licensed psychotherapist in practice for over three decades and worked closely with Carl R. Rogers in La Jolla, California - facilitating encounter groups, large group events and training psychotherapists in many countries. Her recent work explores the present and potential future impacts of global cultural shifts on psychological development and emotional wellbeing. Books include *Em busca da vida*, with C.R. Rogers, J.K. Wood and A. Fonseca (Summus,1983); *Ten Things To Do In A Conceptual Emergency*, with G. Leicester (Triarchy, 2009); and the *Handbook of Person-Centered Psychotherapy and Counselling* with M. Cooper, P. Schmid and G. Wyatt (Palgrave Macmillan, 2008). She is married to Robert Lucas with whom she resides in Carlsbad, California, spending as much time as they can with family in Yorkshire and IFF colleagues at the Boathouse, Aberdour.

Graham Leicester is Director of International Futures Forum. Graham previously ran Scotland's leading think tank, the Scottish Council Foundation, founded in 1997. From 1984-1995 he served as a diplomat in HM Diplomatic Service, specialising in China (he speaks Mandarin Chinese) and the EU. Between 1995 and 1997 he was senior research fellow with the Constitution Unit at University College London. He has also worked as a freelance professional cellist, including with the BBC Concert Orchestra. He has a strong interest in governance, innovation and education, and has previously worked with OECD, the World Bank Institute and other agencies on the themes of governance in a knowledge society and the governance of the long term. He is author of a number of books on themes including transformative innovation and the 21st century competencies.

About Triarchy Press

Triarchy Press is a small, independent publisher of books that bring a wider, systemic or contextual approach to many different areas of life, including:

> Government, Education, Health and other public services
> Ecology, Sustainability and Regenerative Cultures
> Leading and Managing Organizations
> The Money System
> Psychotherapy and Arts and other Expressive Therapies
> Walking, Psychogeography and Mythogeography
> Movement and Somatics
> Innovation
> The Future and Future Studies

> www.triarchypress.net

About IFF

IFF is a charity registered in Scotland with a mission to enable people and organisations to flourish in powerful times. We work with governments, communities, businesses, foundations and individuals. We address complex, messy, seemingly intractable issues – local, global and all levels in between – fostering practical hope and wise initiative. We support people making a difference in the face of all that stands in the way of making a difference, rising to the challenge of the moment. We develop their 21st century competencies for thriving in complexity and their capacity for inspiring and transformative innovation. We offer resources to support this activity through a thriving community Hub, events, workshops, tools, processes, training and other online materials available in the IFF Practice Centre.

internationalfuturesforum.com
iffpraxis.com

About Koreo

Koreo is a learning consultancy dedicated to imagining and building a better world. We create radical learning spaces, programmes & ventures that help us all rise to the demands and urgency of our time. Since 2004 we have become one of the UK's leading learning partners for organisations with a social purpose. As a small, committed team of learning designers and producers, facilitators and coaches, supported by a growing community of specialist associates and partners across the UK, we have worked alongside leaders in communities, supported household name charities to shift culture towards learning and transformation, and brought together networks to collaborate across organisational, sectoral and geographic boundaries.

koreo.co